OUR GOD
IS MARCHING
ON

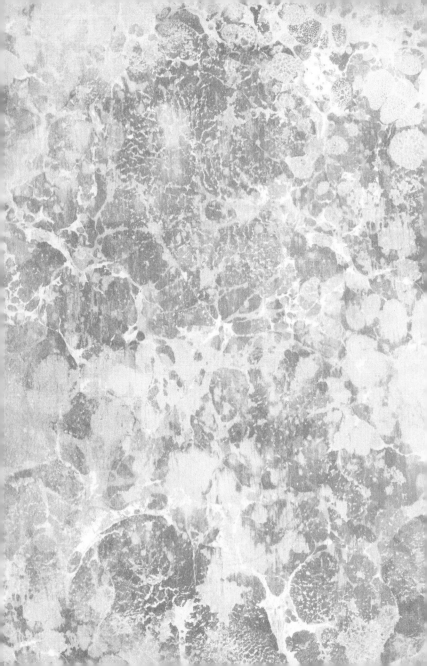

DR. MARTIN LUTHER KING JR.

OUR GOD IS MARCHING ON

Foreword by Clyde W. Ford

**MartinLuther
KingJr.**_Library_

**MartinLuther
KingJr.** *Library*

In Association With INTELLECTUAL PROPERTIES MANAGEMENT, INC.

License granted by Intellectual Properties Management, Inc., Atlanta, GA, exclusive licensor of The King Estate.

HarperCollins books may be purchased for educational, business, or sales promotional use. For information, please email the Special Markets Department at SPsales@harpercollins.com.

Designed by Ralph Fowler
Art © Yulia Koldovska/Shutterstock

Library of Congress Cataloging-in-Publication Data has been applied for.

ISBN 978-0-06-335099-1

24 25 26 27 28 LBC 5 4 3 2 1

Foreword

By all measures, at a little over three minutes, it was a short speech, but it ended a long series of marches at a pivotal moment in the Black American struggle for civil rights. Martin Luther King Jr. delivered "Our God Is Marching On" in the afternoon of March 25, 1965, to twenty-five thousand people on the grounds of the Alabama state capitol to mark the end of the third Selma march.

The *third* Selma march? Yes. It may come as a

surprise that there was not just one march, but three Selma-to-Montgomery marches. Popular belief has conflated these three marches into one. Yet to understand the importance and the gravity of this King speech requires a step back in time to just before the first of those marches.

February 18, 1965, was a day marked by a protest for voting rights, long denied Black citizens of Alabama. Organizing, protests, and civil disobedience in support of voting rights had gone on in Selma and the surrounding area for many months, including a visit by Malcolm X to the Tuskegee Institute, not far from Selma, in support of this campaign. On February 18, Jimmie Lee Jackson, a Black voting rights activist inspired by Martin Luther King, was part of the protest with his sister, mother, and grandfather. When white Alabama state troopers attacked the protest, the family fled into a nearby café. Troopers followed and began beating Jackson's mother. When Jackson attempted to protect her, he was shot by Corporal James Bonard Fowler. Jackson died several days later.

In the aftermath of Jimmie Lee Jackson's death, to defuse the anger and desire for revenge reverberating within the area's Black community, Reverend Hosea Williams of the Southern Christian Leadership Conference (SCLC, pronounced "slick") and John R. Lewis of the Student Nonviolent Coordinating Committee (SNCC, or "snick") led protesters on a march from Selma to Montgomery on Sunday, March 7, 1965. Martin Luther King Jr. was not among them. The protesters wanted to meet with Alabama governor and avowed segregationist George Wallace about Jackson's death. In Selma, the seat of Dallas County, Alabama, Sheriff Jim Clark had ordered all white men over the age of twenty-one to be deputized prior to the March 7 march. When protesters crossed over the Edmund Pettus Bridge to the Montgomery side, they were met by a line of Alabama state troopers and deputized white men, who beat them mercilessly in what has become known as Bloody Sunday. John Lewis suffered a skull fracture and scars that he bore for the rest of his life.

President Lyndon B. Johnson, labor leader Walter Reuther, all frontline civil rights organizations, and many others swiftly and roundly condemned Bloody Sunday. King stepped in to the planning for the second Selma march, which was to be held on March 9 to protest the police violence witnessed in the first march and to continue advocating for voting rights. SCLC sought a restraining order preventing state troopers from using violence against protesters. But instead of issuing that order, US District Court judge Frank

Johnson issued a temporary restraining order against the protesters seeking to hold a march. With John Lewis recovering from his injuries, James Forman of SNCC and Hosea Williams, breaking with SCLC, argued that the march must be held in violation of Judge Johnson's order, even though many in SCLC believed that Judge Johnson was waiting for federal assurances that a restraining order against state troopers would be enforced.

King attempted to broker a compromise between those advocating for a march and those who wanted to wait for the judge's final order. On Tuesday, March 9, King led a group of protesters from Selma on a route prearranged with local white authorities; he prayed with the protesters but then turned them around and marched back to Selma without crossing the Edmund Pettus Bridge in what became known as Turnaround Tuesday. That evening, three white Unitarian Universalist ministers were severely beaten with clubs by members of the Selma KKK. James Reeb, one of the three, died two days later from the injuries he sustained.

Selma had now become a powder keg. SNCC and SCLC were at loggerheads over the tactics of Turnaround Tuesday and whether it represented capitulation or strategic retreat. King's leadership and the nonviolent methods he advocated were directly challenged by a younger generation of activists. President Johnson's attempts to strong-arm Governor Wallace into allowing another march were unsuccessful, so the president gave Judge Johnson his guarantee of federal enforcement. On March 17, Judge Johnson lifted his restraining order.

King then led the third Selma march, planned for

March 21 to 24, 1965. On Sunday, the first day of the march, almost eight thousand people from around the world departed the Brown Chapel AME Church in Selma to begin the fifty-four-mile march to Montgomery, escorted by members of the Alabama National Guard, since federalized by President Johnson. From this march came the iconic photograph of Martin Luther King Jr. walking hand in hand with his wife, Coretta, and arm in arm with Ralph Abernathy, along with Juanita Abernathy, Fred Shuttlesworth, Ralph Bunche, Rabbi Abraham Joshua Heschel, and many others. But it is little-reported that on March 23, hundreds of Black marchers donned yarmulkes, Jewish skullcaps, in support and admiration for Rabbi Heschel and Rabbi Maurice Davis at the head of the march. The yarmulkes became known as "freedom caps."

Harry Belafonte, Sammy Davis Jr., Nina Simone,

Joan Baez, Tony Bennett, Peter, Paul and Mary, and a star-studded list of entertainers performed for the marchers on the evening of March 24 as they camped on the outskirts of Montgomery. The next day, twenty-five thousand people marched from the encampment to the steps of the Alabama state capitol building, where King delivered the speech contained in this book.

Like the bridge that the marchers crossed getting to the state capitol, "Our God Is Marching On" is itself a bridge. It is a bridge inviting white Americans, particularly poor white Americans, to understand how racism has historically manipulated them. "If it may be said of the slavery era that the white man took the world and gave the Negro Jesus," King orates, "then it may be said of the Reconstruction era that the Southern aristocracy took the world and gave the poor white man Jim Crow. He gave him Jim Crow. And when his wrinkled stomach cried out for the food that his empty pockets could not provide, he ate Jim Crow, a psychological bird that told him that no matter how bad off he was, at least he was a white man, better than the Black man."

King's speech is a bridge offering Black Americans, fearful of nonviolence in the face of the recalcitrant violence of whites, a means of leaving those fears behind. "And so I plead with you this afternoon as we go ahead: remain committed to nonviolence. Our aim must never be to defeat or humiliate the white man but to win his friendship and understanding," King says.

King's speech is a bridge for all to understand that police violence and denial of voting rights will not stand in a democracy, and to understand how these two issues are deeply entwined. "Let us march on ballot boxes, march on ballot boxes until race-baiters disappear from the political arena. Let us march on ballot boxes until the salient misdeeds of blood-thirsty mobs will be transformed into the calculated good deeds of orderly citizens. Let us march on ballot boxes until the Wallaces of our nation tremble away in silence."

But King's words are also a bridge to an unseen future he never lived long enough to witness. Paraphrasing the nineteenth-century abolitionist Theodore Parker, King says in this speech, "The arc of the moral universe is long, but it bends toward justice." Who cannot hear future Black president Barack Obama's elocution of that same phrase in his own orations?

How long until we as a society, a nation, a world cross that bridge to reach the end of that arc, King asks the crowd. "Not long!" he replies, and the audience echoes him many times. Here in this marvelously framed short speech, sometimes called the "How Long? Not Long!" speech, is a bridge for us all. Please, read this speech not just as a historical reference to a time gone by but also as a call to action now. Reducing police violence. Expanding voting rights. Meeting racism and hatred with love and nonviolence. The very issues protesters marched for in Selma in March 1965—the very issues at the heart of King's speech—are still with us today.

This speech, and its historical backstory, put forth the question, "What Edmund Pettus Bridge is each of us called on to cross in order to bring about fundamental changes within ourselves and within society?" Is it the bridge from nonvoting to voting? Is it the bridge from castigating the strangers among us to welcoming them as brothers and sisters? Is it the bridge from violent retribution in the face of differences to nonviolent resolution of those differences? How we answer these questions, and how we act on our answers, will measure how well we have read and taken to heart the words Martin Luther King Jr. spoke in this short speech, "Our God Is Marching On."

—Clyde W. Ford

Director, The Martin Luther King Jr.

Library Project at HarperCollins Publishers

"OUR GOD IS MARCHING ON" SPEECH

March 25, 1965
Montgomery, Alabama

My dear abiding friends, Ralph Abernathy, and to all the distinguished Americans seated here on the rostrum.

My friends and co-workers of the state of Alabama,

and to all of the freedom-loving

people who have assembled here this

afternoon, from all over our nation

and from all over the world.

Last Sunday, more than
eight thousand of us started on a
mighty walk from Selma, Alabama.
We have walked through desolate
valleys and across trying hills,
we have walked on meandering
highways and rested our bodies
on rocky byways.

Some of our faces are burned

from the outpourings of

the sweltering sun.

Some have literally

slept in the mud.

We have been drenched

by the rains.

Our bodies are tired, and

our feet are somewhat sore.

But today as I stand before you and think back over that great march, I can say as Sister Pollard said, a seventy-year-old Negro woman who lived in this community during the bus boycott. One day she was asked while walking if she wanted a ride and when she answered, "No," the person said, "Well, aren't you tired?"

And with her ungrammatical
profundity, she said, "My feets is tired,
but my soul is rested."

And in a real sense this afternoon,
we can say that our feet are
tired, but our souls are rested.

They told us we wouldn't get here.

And there were those who said
that we would get here only
over their dead bodies.

But all the world today knows

that we are here and that

we are standing before the forces

of power in the state of Alabama

saying, "We ain't goin' to let

nobody turn us around."

Now it is not an accident that
one of the great marches of
American history should terminate
in Montgomery, Alabama.

Just ten years ago in this very city,
a new philosophy was born
of the Negro's struggle.

Montgomery was the first city
in the South in which the entire
Negro community united and swore to
face their age-old oppressors.

Out of its struggle, more than
bus segregation was won.

A new idea, more powerful than guns or clubs was born.

Negroes took it and carried it across the South in epic battles that electrified the nation and the world.

And yet strangely the climactic conflicts were always fought and won on Alabama soil.

After Montgomery's, heroic confrontations loomed up in Mississippi, Arkansas, Georgia, and elsewhere. But not until the colossus of segregation was challenged in Birmingham did the conscience of America begin to bleed.

White America was profoundly
aroused by Birmingham,
because it witnessed a whole
community of Negroes facing terror
and brutality with majestic,
strong, and heroic courage.

From the wells of its democratic spirit,

the nation finally forced Congress to

write legislation in the hopes it would

eradicate the stain of Birmingham.

The Civil Rights Act of 1964 gave Negroes some part of their rightful dignity, but without the vote it was dignity without strength.

Once more the method of
nonviolent resistance was unsheathed
from its scabbard and once again
an entire community was mobilized
to confront the adversary. And
again the brutality of a dying order
shrieks across the land.

Yet Selma, Alabama,

became a shining moment in

the conscience of man.

If the worst of American life

lurked in its dark streets,

the best of Americans rose passionately

across the nation to overcome it.

There never was a moment in
American history more honorable
and more inspiring than the
pilgrimage of clergymen and laymen
of every race and faith pouring
into Selma to face danger at the
side of its embattled Negroes.

Confrontation of good and evil
compressed in the tiny community
of Selma generated the massive
power to turn the whole nation
to a new course.

A president born in the South had the sensitivity to feel the will of the country, and in an address that will live in history as one of the most passionate pleas for human rights ever made by a president of our nation, he pledged the might of the federal government to cast off the centuries-old blight.

President Johnson rightly praised
the courage of the Negro for awakening
the conscience of the nation.

On our part we must pay our profound respects to the white Americans who cherish their democratic traditions over the ugly customs and privileges of generations and come forth boldly to join hands with us.

From Montgomery to Birmingham,

from Birmingham to Selma,

from Selma back to Montgomery,

a trail wound in a circle long and

often bloody, yet it has become a

highway up from darkness.

Alabama has tried to nurture and defend evil, but the evil is choking to death in the dusty roads and streets of this state.

So I stand before you this afternoon with the conviction that segregation is on its deathbed in Alabama and the only thing uncertain about it is how costly the segregationists and Wallace will make the funeral.

Our whole campaign in
Alabama has been centered around
the right to vote.

In focusing the attention of the nation and the world today on the flagrant denial of the right to vote, we are exposing the very origin, the root cause, of racial segregation in the Southland.

Racial segregation as a way of life did not come about as a natural result of hatred between the races immediately after the Civil War.

There were no laws segregating the races then. As the noted historian, C. Vann Woodward, in his book, *The Strange Career of Jim Crow*, clearly points out, the segregation of the races was really a political stratagem employed by the emerging Bourbon interests in the South to keep the Southern masses divided and Southern labor the cheapest in the land.

You see, it was a simple thing to keep the poor white masses working for near-starvation wages in the years that followed the Civil War.

Why, if the poor white plantation or mill worker became dissatisfied with his low wages, the plantation or mill owner would merely threaten to fire him and hire former Negro slaves and pay him even less. Thus, the Southern wage level was kept almost unbearably low.

Toward the end of the
Reconstruction era, something very
significant happened.

That is what was known as the Populist Movement. The leaders of this movement began awakening the poor white masses and the former Negro slaves to the fact that they were being fleeced by the emerging Bourbon interests.

Not only that, but they began uniting the Negro and white masses into a voting bloc that threatened to drive the Bourbon interests from the command posts of political power in the South.

To meet this threat, the Southern aristocracy began immediately to engineer this development of a segregated society. I want you to follow me through here because this is very important to see the roots of racism and the denial of the right to vote.

Through their control of mass media, they revised the doctrine of white supremacy. They saturated the thinking of the poor white masses with it, thus clouding their minds to the real issue involved in the Populist Movement.

They then directed the placement

on the books of the South of laws

that made it a crime for Negroes

and whites to come together

as equals at any level.

And that did it. That crippled and eventually destroyed the Populist Movement of the nineteenth century.

If it may be said of the slavery era that the white man took the world and gave the Negro Jesus, then it may be said of the Reconstruction era that the Southern aristocracy took the world and gave the poor white man Jim Crow.

He gave him Jim Crow. And when his wrinkled stomach cried out for the food that his empty pockets could not provide, he ate Jim Crow, a psychological bird that told him that no matter how bad off he was, at least he was a white man, better than the Black man.

And he ate Jim Crow. And when
his undernourished children
cried out for the necessities that his
low wages could not provide,
he showed them the Jim Crow signs
on the buses and in the stores, on the
streets and in the public buildings.

And his children, too, learned to feed upon Jim Crow, their last outpost of psychological oblivion. Thus the threat of the free exercise of the ballot by the Negro and the white masses alike resulted in the establishing of a segregated society.

They segregated Southern money from the poor whites; they segregated Southern mores from the rich whites; they segregated Southern churches from Christianity; they segregated Southern minds from honest thinking; and they segregated the Negro from everything.

That's what happened when the Negro and white masses of the South threatened to unite and build a great society: a society of justice where none would prey upon the weakness of others; a society of plenty where greed and poverty would be done away; a society of brotherhood where every man would respect the dignity and worth of human personality.

We have come a long way since

that travesty of justice was perpetrated

upon the American mind.

James Weldon Johnson put it

eloquently. He said:

"We have come over a way

That with tears hath

been watered.

We have come treading our paths

Through the blood of
the slaughtered.

Out of the gloomy past,

Till now we stand at last

Where the white gleam

Of our bright star is cast."

Today I want to tell the city of Selma,

today I want to say to the state of

Alabama, today I want to say

to the people of America and the

nations of the world: We are not

about to turn around.

We are on the move now.

Yes, we are on the move and no
wave of racism can stop us.

We are on the move now.

The burning of our churches
will not deter us.

We are on the move now.

The bombing of our homes
will not dissuade us.

We are on the move now.

The beating and killing of our clergymen and young people will not divert us.

We are on the move now.

The wanton release of their known murderers would not discourage us.

We are on the move now.

Like an idea whose time has come,

not even the marching of

mighty armies can halt us.

We are moving to the
land of freedom.

Let us therefore continue our
triumph and march to the
realization of the American dream.

Let us march on
segregated housing.

Until every ghetto of social and
economic depression dissolves and
Negroes and whites live side by side in
decent, safe, and sanitary housing.

Let us march on
segregated schools.

Until every vestige of segregated
and inferior education becomes a thing
of the past and Negroes and whites
study side by side in the socially healing
context of the classroom.

Let us march on poverty,

until no American parent

has to skip a meal so that their

children may eat. March on

poverty, until no starved man

walks the streets of our cities

and towns in search of jobs

that do not exist.

Let us march on poverty
until wrinkled stomachs in Mississippi
are filled, and the idle industries of
Appalachia are realized and revitalized,
and broken lives in sweltering ghettos
are mended and remolded.

Let us march on ballot boxes,

march on ballot boxes until

race-baiters disappear from

the political arena.

Let us march on ballot boxes
until the salient misdeeds of
bloodthirsty mobs will be
transformed into the calculated good
deeds of orderly citizens.

Let us march on ballot boxes

until the Wallaces of our nation

tremble away in silence.

Let us march on ballot boxes,
until we send to our city councils,
state legislatures, and the
United States Congress, men who
will not fear to do justice,
love mercy, and walk humbly
with their God.

Let us march on ballot boxes
until brotherhood becomes more
than a meaningless word in
an opening prayer, but the order of the
day on every legislative agenda.

Let us march on ballot boxes
until all over Alabama God's children
will be able to walk the earth in
decency and honor.

There is nothing wrong
with marching in this sense.

The Bible tells us that the mighty men
of Joshua merely walked about the
walled city of Jericho and the barriers to
freedom came tumbling down.

I like that old Negro spiritual,
"Joshua Fit the Battle of Jericho."
In its simple, yet colorful, depiction
of that great moment in biblical
history, it tells us that:

"Joshua fit the battle of Jericho,

Joshua fit the battle of Jericho,

And the walls come

tumbling down.

Up to the walls of Jericho

they marched, spear in hand.

'Go blow them ram horns,'

Joshua cried,

''Cause the battle am in my hand.'"

These words I have given you

just as they were given us by

the unknown, long-dead,

dark-skinned originator.

Some now long-gone Black bard

bequeathed to posterity these words in

ungrammatical form, yet with emphatic

pertinence for all of us today.

The battle is in our hands.
And we can answer with creative
nonviolence the call to higher ground
to which the new directions of our
struggle summons us. The road ahead
is not altogether a smooth one. There
are no broad highways that lead us
easily and inevitably to quick solutions.

But we must keep going.

In the glow of the lamplight

on my desk a few nights ago,

I gazed again upon the wondrous

sign of our times, full of hope and

promise of the future.

And I smiled to see in the

newspaper photographs of

many a decade ago, the faces so bright,

so solemn, of our valiant heroes, the

people of Montgomery.

To this list may be added
the names of all those who have
fought and, yes, died in the
nonviolent army of our day:

Medgar Evers,

Three civil rights workers

in Mississippi last summer,

William Moore,

as has already been mentioned,

the Reverend James Reeb,

Jimmie Lee Jackson,

and four little girls in the

church of God in Birmingham

on Sunday morning.

But in spite of this, we must go on and be sure that they did not die in vain. The pattern of their feet as they walked through Jim Crow barriers in the great stride toward freedom is the thunder of the marching men of Joshua, and the world rocks beneath their tread.

My people, my people, listen.

The battle is in our hands.

The battle is in our hands

in Mississippi and Alabama

and all over the United States.

I know there is a cry today in

Alabama, we see it in

numerous editorials:

"When will Martin Luther King,
SCLC, SNCC, and all of these
civil rights agitators and all of the white
clergymen and labor leaders
and students and others get out
of our community and let Alabama
return to normalcy?"

But I have a message that
I would like to leave with
Alabama this evening.

That is exactly what we don't want,
and we will not allow it to happen, for
we know that it was normalcy
in Marion that led to the brutal
murder of Jimmie Lee Jackson.

It was normalcy in Birmingham
that led to the murder on Sunday
morning of four beautiful,
unoffending, innocent girls.

It was normalcy on Highway 80

that led state troopers to use tear gas

and horses and billy clubs against

unarmed human beings who were

simply marching for justice.

It was normalcy by a café in Selma,
Alabama, that led to the brutal beating
of Reverend James Reeb.

It is normalcy all over our country which leaves the Negro perishing on a lonely island of poverty in the midst of a vast ocean of material prosperity. It is normalcy all over Alabama that prevents the Negro from becoming a registered voter.

No, we will not allow Alabama to return to normalcy.

The only normalcy that we will settle for is the normalcy that recognizes the dignity and worth of all of God's children.

The only normalcy that we will settle for is the normalcy that allows judgment to run down like waters, and righteousness like a mighty stream. The only normalcy that we will settle for is the normalcy of brotherhood, the normalcy of true peace, the normalcy of justice.

So as we go away this afternoon,
let us go away more than ever before
committed to the struggle and
committed to nonviolence.

I must admit to you there are
still some difficulties ahead.

We are still in for a season of
suffering in many of the
Black Belt counties of Alabama,
many areas of Mississippi,
many areas of Louisiana.

I must admit to you there are
still jail cells waiting for us,
dark and difficult moments.

We will go on with the faith

that nonviolence and its power

transformed dark yesterdays into

bright tomorrows. We will be able

to change all of these conditions.

And so I plead with you this afternoon as we go ahead: remain committed to nonviolence.

Our aim must never be to defeat or humiliate the white man but to win his friendship and understanding.

We must come to see that the end we seek is a society at peace with itself, a society that can live with its conscience. That will be a day not of the white man, not of the Black man. That will be the day of man as man.

I know you are asking today,

"How long will it take?"

Somebody's asking,

"How long will prejudice blind

the visions of men, darken their

understanding, and drive bright-eyed

wisdom from her sacred throne?"

Somebody's asking,
"When will wounded justice,
lying prostrate on the streets of Selma
and Birmingham and communities
all over the South, be lifted from this
dust of shame to reign supreme
among the children of men?"

Somebody's asking,

"When will the radiant star of hope

be plunged against the nocturnal

bosom of this lonely night,

plucked from weary souls with

chains of fear and the manacles of

death? How long will justice be

crucified, and truth bear it?"

I come to say to you this afternoon,

however difficult the moment,

however frustrating the hour,

it will not be long, because "truth

crushed to earth will rise again."

How long? Not long, because

"no lie can live forever."

How long? Not long, because

"you shall reap what you sow."

How long? Not long:

"Truth forever on the scaffold,

Wrong forever on the throne,

Yet that scaffold sways the future,

And, behind the dim unknown,

Standeth God within the shadow,

Keeping watch above his own."

How long? Not long,

because the arc of the moral universe is

long, but it bends toward justice.

How long? Not long, because:

"Mine eyes have seen the glory of the
coming of the Lord;

He is trampling out the vintage where
the grapes of wrath are stored;

He has loosed the fateful lightning

of his terrible swift sword;

His truth is marching on.

He has sounded forth the trumpet

that shall never call retreat;

He is sifting out the hearts of men

before His judgment seat.

O, be swift, my soul, to answer Him!

Be jubilant my feet!

Our God is marching on.

Glory, hallelujah!

Glory, hallelujah!

Glory, hallelujah!

Glory, hallelujah!

His truth is marching on."

About Martin Luther King Jr.

Dr. Martin Luther King Jr. (1929–1968), civil rights leader and recipient of the Nobel Prize for Peace, inspired and sustained the struggle for freedom, nonviolence, interracial brotherhood, and social justice.

About Clyde W. Ford

Clyde W. Ford is a diversity, equity, and inclusion consultant who has met with the CEOs of Microsoft and IBM and is the current director of the MLK Library Project at HarperCollins. He's presented hundreds of talks and trainings for colleges and universities, private corporations, and civic groups in the United States, Canada, and Europe. An award-winning author of more than a dozen books, Clyde's been a featured guest on *The Oprah Winfrey Show*, *Good Morning America*, NPR, C-SPAN/BookTV, and numerous radio and television programs across the country.